Fire Timeline

ca. 1 Million Years Ago

Possible human-controlled fire at Wonderwerk Cave, South Africa.

ca. 7500 BCE

Copper is smelted (extracted from its ore by heating) and annealed (heated to make it easier to work with and shape).

ca. 70,000 Years Ago

First lamps invented: hollow, natural objects filled with fuel and ignited.

ca. 240,000–225,000 Years Ago

Earliest evidence of hearths in Europe, in Bolomor Cave, Spain.

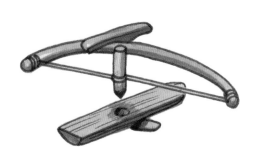

ca. 40,000–20,000 Years Ago

Earth ovens and kilns developed, clay pots fired.

80s BCE

Roman politician and businessman Marcus Licinius Crassus establishes the world's first fire brigade.

1926

Robert Goddard launches the first successful liquid-fuel rocket.

1728

The first cast-iron stoves are built.

9th Century BCE

Fire used as a weapon by the Assyrians, who fired flaming arrows and pots at their enemies.

1886

Karl Benz is the first to patent a car powered by an internal combustion engine.

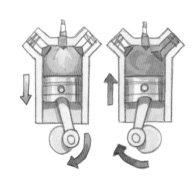

1712 CE

Thomas Newcomen invents the first practical steam engine.

The Fire Triangle

The main source of oxygen is the air, which contains 21% oxygen. Plants give out oxygen as a waste product.

Heat can come from a flame or a spark, or from the Sun.

OXYGEN

HEAT

FUEL

Fuel can be anything that will burn, including natural gas, gasoline, coal, wood, or paper.

Oxygen, heat, and fuel are often called the "fire triangle." All three of these elements are required for a fire to occur. This is useful knowledge for firefighters, because a fire can be prevented or extinguished by removing one of these elements. For example, covering a fire with a fire blanket will keep out oxygen, and this will put out the fire.

To stay safe from fire, it's important to keep fuel sources, such as paper, wood, and gasoline, away from heat sources, such as matches.

Author:

Alex Woolf studied history at Essex University, England. He is the author of over 80 books for children. Recent titles include *You Wouldn't Want to Live Without Books!* and *You Wouldn't Want to Be in the Trenches in World War One!* He also writes fiction for children and young adults.

Artist:

Mark Bergin was born in Hastings, England, in 1961. He studied at Eastbourne College of Art and has specialized in historical reconstructions as well as aviation and maritime subjects since 1983. He lives in Bexhill-on-Sea with his wife and three children.

Series creator:

David Salariya was born in Dundee, Scotland. He has illustrated a wide range of books and has created and designed many new series for publishers in the UK and overseas. David established The Salariya Book Company in 1989. He lives in Brighton with his wife, illustrator Shirley Willis, and their son, Jonathan.

Editor: **Stephen Haynes**

Editorial Assistant: **Mark Williams**

Published in Great Britain in 2015 by
The Salariya Book Company Ltd
25 Marlborough Place, Brighton BN1 1UB

ISBN-13: 978-0-531-21364-3 (lib. bdg.) 978-0-531-21407-7 (pbk.)

All rights reserved.
Published in 2015 in the United States
by Franklin Watts
An imprint of Scholastic Inc.
Published simultaneously in Canada.

A CIP catalog record for this book is available
from the Library of Congress.

Printed and bound in China.
Printed on paper from sustainable sources.

1 2 3 4 5 6 7 8 9 10 R 24 23 22 21 20 19 18 17 16 15

PAPER FROM
SUSTAINABLE
FORESTS

You Wouldn't Want to Live Without™
Fire!

Written by
Alex Woolf

Illustrated by
Mark Bergin

Created and designed by
David Salariya

Franklin Watts®
An Imprint of Scholastic Inc.
NEW YORK • TORONTO • LONDON • AUCKLAND • SYDNEY
MEXICO CITY • NEW DELHI • HONG KONG
DANBURY, CONNECTICUT

Contents

Introduction

We see fire whenever we light a match or turn on a gas stove. But there are many more indirect ways in which fire plays a part in our lives. For example, fire can make electricity. Fire makes cars go and planes fly, and it's needed to make things like pottery, plastic, metal, and glass. Fire has made our world—yet we hardly notice it.

Fire has always existed in nature, long before humans discovered it. The Sun itself is often thought of as a giant ball of fire. Fire can also occur naturally here on Earth—for example, when lava from a volcanic eruption sets vegetation on fire.

Fire must have been terrifying to early humans. It was destructive and dangerous—something to run away from. But eventually we learned how to create it for ourselves and control it. This was a major turning point in human history. In this book we look at some of the ways in which fire has transformed human society.

Warning

DON'T PLAY WITH FIRE! Fire can be fun to look at, and you may be tempted to touch a lit candle or set something on fire. **Don't do it!** Children who play with fire can end up burning themselves, hurting other people, and destroying property.

How Would You Survive Without Fire?

Imagine living in a world before the conquest of fire. In the winter months you are constantly cold. The food you eat is raw and tough to digest. The day always ends at sunset. And in the long hours of darkness, you and your people are at the mercy of wild animals.

Then, one stormy night, you see a lightning bolt strike a tree. The tree bursts into flame. It's a scary sight—as if part of the Sun has escaped from the sky and fallen to Earth—but it's also intriguing. What if you could steal some of this strange, hot, bright stuff for yourself? It might just change your life…

Scary stuff! But it could be useful…

What Is Fire?

Oxygen — Heat — Fuel

FIRE IS A CHEMICAL REACTION between an ignited material, or fuel (such as wood), and oxygen. The reaction gives off heat, flames, and smoke. So to start a fire you need three things: fuel, heat, and oxygen.

WHO FIRST TAMED FIRE? We don't know, but there is evidence of ash and charred bone in a cave in South Africa dating back a million years.

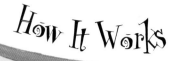

To make the spindle turn faster, loop string around it and attach this to the ends of a curved stick. You now have a bow-drill. Move the bow from side to side to turn the spindle.

Pad or handle
Bow
Spindle
Board

MAKING FIRE. Early humans relied on lightning to make fire. Later, they learned how to make fire for themselves using friction, by twisting a wooden spindle inside a hole in a larger piece of wood (below left).

PROMET...
importan...
it. Th...
Prome...
and gave...

Spindle or "drill"

You said you were good at this.

Fire board

Would You Like a Little Light?

You are a member of a people living in Africa about a million years ago. Your people have learned how to make fire. You are no longer forced to go to bed when the Sun goes away. Every evening, you gather wood from the forest and light a big fire in the mouth of your cave. You gather around it and tell stories.

The night feels safer and brighter now. The animals that used to threaten you are scared of the fire and stay away. And when you go hunting, you can even take fire with you—in the form of a glowing wooden ember. It helps you find your way home in the dark.

THE FIRST LAMP was invented around 70,000 years ago. Someone filled a hollow rock or shell with moss soaked in animal fat, and lit it.

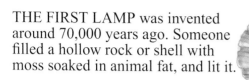

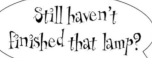

Still haven't finished that lamp?

No, it's too dark to see what I'm doing.

How It Works

The Argand lamp, invented in 1780, was a huge step forward for oil lamps, providing a much brighter, steadier flame. A cylindrical metal tube around the wick allowed air into the center of the burner, and a glass chimney increased the draft, so more of the oil burned.

Chimney

THE ANCIENT GREEKS made clay lamps, first on a pottery wheel (above), and then in molds to allow mass production.

This will impress the emperor!

THOMAS EDISON AND JOSEPH SWAN came up with the electric lightbulb almost simultaneously in the 1870s. Electricity flows through a filament (fine wire) inside the bulb, heating it so it radiates light.

EARLY CANDLES were made in China around 200 BCE from whale fat with a rice-paper wick. The Chinese also used animal fat and beeswax.

GAS LIGHTING began in 1792 when William Murdoch used coal gas to light his house. Soon city streets were lit by gaslight.

Gas lamp   *Lamplighter*

Edison   *Swan*

Could You Cope Without Cooking?

Now picture yourself about 500,000 years ago, in China. One day, you venture into the charred wilderness of a recently burned forest. Amid the ashes, you find the remains of a deer. The fire has softened the meat and made it tastier and easier to chew. This gives you an idea. A few days later, you bring home some fish. You build a fire and skewer the fish, then hold it over the flames. The smell of the heating fish is enticing. The outside gets a little burned, but the flesh almost melts in your mouth. Delicious! You and your family sleep very well that night.

Well, what did you expect?

Ow! It's hot!

It's burnt!

Smells nice, though!

ROASTING was the first type of cooking. It may have been discovered by accident when someone dropped food into the fire. Cooking fires first appeared around 500,000 years ago.

Cooking causes chemical changes in food. Protein molecules in meat and eggs change shape, altering the appearance and texture. When a potato is heated, cell walls break, making it softer.

BAKING AND BOILING soon followed (left). Food was cooked in pits in the ground or in water-filled rock holes, heated with hot stones.

ANIMAL STOMACHS were among the first cooking containers; they were waterproof and heatproof enough to be boiled or hung over a fire (right). They were followed by leather, pottery, and then bronze vessels.

Cooker Evolution

PRESENT DAY: microwave oven (invented 1946) and TV dinner (invented 1953)

MIDDLE AGES: wood-burning oven

1728: cast-iron oven

1826: gas oven

1882: electric oven

Do You Hanker for Some Heat?

It's now about 42,000 BCE. Your people have been driven from home in Africa by another, more aggressive people. You migrate northward, to a strange, new land that will one day be called Europe, far beyond the familiar horizons of your childhood. Here you must learn to hunt new animals, like the fierce mammoth. And you must get used to a colder climate and long, harsh winters. If it weren't for the precious gift of fire, you could not survive in this place. Thanks to fire, you have been able to travel far from the lands of your ancestors, far away from those who would threaten you and your people. Each night you gather close to the fire. You feel its heat, and give thanks.

FOR THOUSANDS OF YEARS, homes were heated by open fires in the middle of the room, with an opening in the roof to let out the smoke.

Top Tip

Fire heats your water, too, making it easier to keep yourself clean. But heating water for a bath uses a lot of energy, as well as water. Why not take a shower instead?

Heat, but no smoke. Perfect!

That's progress!

HYPOCAUSTS. The ancient Romans invented an early central heating system (above). Air heated by furnaces was conducted through empty spaces under floors and out of pipes in the walls.

CHIMNEYS began appearing in homes around the 12th century CE. Hearths moved from the center of the room to against the wall, and houses became a lot less smoky.

CENTRAL HEATING made a comeback in the 19th century. Water, heated by a furnace, was sent around the building through pipes and radiators.

Could You Be Creative With Clay?

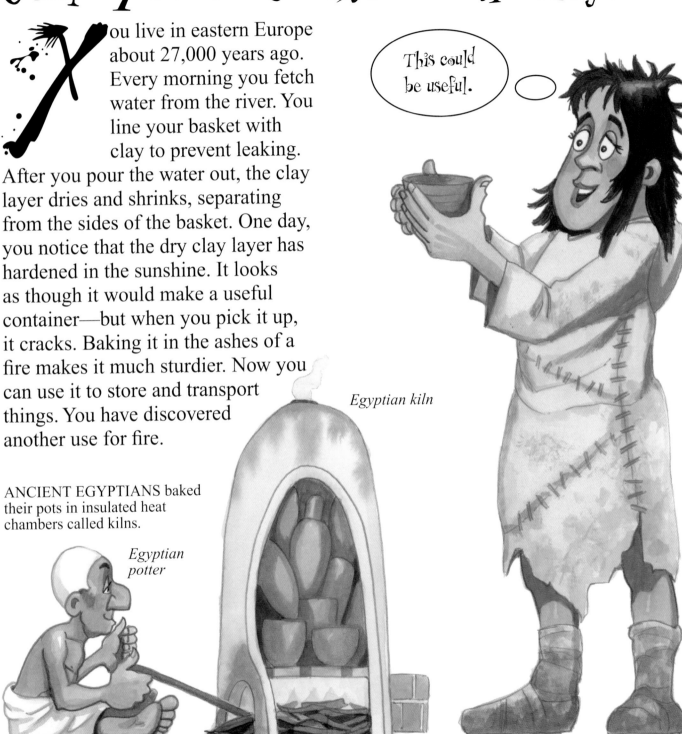

You live in eastern Europe about 27,000 years ago. Every morning you fetch water from the river. You line your basket with clay to prevent leaking. After you pour the water out, the clay layer dries and shrinks, separating from the sides of the basket. One day, you notice that the dry clay layer has hardened in the sunshine. It looks as though it would make a useful container—but when you pick it up, it cracks. Baking it in the ashes of a fire makes it much sturdier. Now you can use it to store and transport things. You have discovered another use for fire.

This could be useful.

ANCIENT EGYPTIANS baked their pots in insulated heat chambers called kilns.

Egyptian kiln

Egyptian potter

Adobe

Cob

Cordwood and mortar

Wattle and daub

Bricks and mortar

Baked clay tiles

WEATHERPROOF. For thousands of years, builders have mixed clay with other materials, then baked it with fire or dried it in the sunshine.

Top Tip

To make your own pot, take a ball of polymer clay—the kind that hardens without baking—and roll it into a thin sausage shape. Coil it around the base of an empty plastic food container. Add more clay, gradually working your way up to the top of the container.

VERSATILE. Clay can be carved or molded into any shape before it is fired. It's been used to make sculpture, musical instruments, tobacco pipes, and slingshot pellets. Some ancient civilizations even wrote on clay tablets.

Please be careful with it.

Trust me!

Greek potter

Greek sculptor

15

Could You Turn a Forest Into a Farm?

ast-forward to Mesopotamia about 8,000 years ago. Your people have learned how to grow plants for food and raise goats for their milk and meat. You no longer have to travel from place to place to hunt animals or gather wild plants. You can settle down in one place and farm the land. But now your community is growing in number, and you need more land for your crops and animals. The fertile river valley where you have settled is covered in forest. You decide to chop down an area of forest, then use fire to burn the fallen trees to clear more land for farming.

Time to get out of here!

You're telling me!

SLASH-AND-BURN. Wandering peoples chopped down and burned areas of forest for farming, until the soil was exhausted. Then they would move on. After a few decades, when the forest had recovered, a new family would move in to slash and burn. This pattern of shifting agriculture continued for thousands of years.

This is easier than hunting fierce animals.

Top Tip

Remember to cut down your forest a few months before the dry season starts. The "slash" then dries out slowly and is ready for burning in the dry season.

IMPROVING THE SOIL. Ash from the burned forest was used to fertilize the soil so that it was ready for planting at the start of the next rainy season.

FIRE-STICK FARMING. Aboriginal Australians burned forests to drive game, such as kangaroos, from cover, and to encourage growth of edible plants.

FIRE PINES are trees that depend on fire to reproduce. Their cones are held together by a sticky resin, which melts in the heat of a fire, releasing the seeds.

17

Does Your Forge Need Fire?

You are a metalworker living in Persia around 2000 BCE. You extract copper from green crystals of malachite, dug from the ground and crushed into powder. You light a fire and sprinkle the powder on the hot coals. You use bellows to blow air into the fire, raising the temperature. Two hours pass. Changes in the color of the flames tell you the copper has been smelted. You place the copper fragments in a crucible (vessel) and melt them, combined with small amounts of tin, to make bronze. You work the heated bronze to make tools, jewelry, and weapons.

Keep going or you'll be fired!

Working bronze

I'm sure the malachite's been fired for long enough now.

Ancient pot bellows

COPPER, TIN, AND LEAD were the first metals to be smelted and worked using fire. Copper was too soft to be made into edged tools, but adding tin made the harder alloy, bronze.

Tongs

Crucible

I just bought this bronze sword, and now you're saying I should upgrade to iron?

The forge must not get too hot or too cool. The smith controls the temperature by using bellows to adjust the flow of air to the fire.

THREE AGES. The discovery of metals was so important to civilization that we divide human prehistory into Stone Age, Bronze Age, and Iron Age.

GLASS is another material made using fire. It's a mixture of sand and other minerals, melted together at very high temperatures.

Hammer

Tongs

Anvil

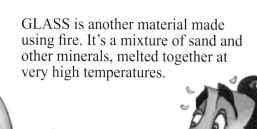

Glassblower

THE FORGE is the hearth for heating metals so they can be worked. The smith grips the heated metal with tongs and uses a hammer and anvil to shape it.

Do You Fancy Being a Firefighter?

The year is 80 BCE. The place: Rome. You are employed by wealthy businessman Marcus Licinius Crassus as a member of the world's first fire brigade. Your boss isn't extinguishing fires just out of kindness, though—he wants money for it. When you reach the scene of a fire, you have to wait while the house owner agrees to Crassus's price for putting the fire out. If he doesn't agree, you simply stand there and watch the building burn. Sometimes the desperate owner eventually agrees to pay, but by then the price has gone up.

Once the building has burned down, crafty Crassus buys it up for a fraction of its original value.

This is how Crassus came to own so much of Rome.

I can't pay that much!

Well, that's my final offer.

BEFORE THE 1600s, fires were usually fought by citizen volunteers with buckets and hand pumps.

FIRE ENGINES appeared in the 1700s. They were tubs of water on wheels that were hauled to the fire (left). A hand-powered pump sent water squirting through a hose.

TODAY'S FIRE BRIGADES (right) are made up of highly trained personnel. They are equipped to handle all types of fire emergencies.

WILDFIRES are fought by building firebreaks around them (below right). Backfires are started to burn up fuel in the wildfire's path.

Can You Fight With Fire?

You are a captain of the Byzantine navy in 678 CE, fighting the Arabs who are besieging your home city of Constantinople. An enemy ship comes near. Soldiers are preparing to board your vessel. It is time to try out a brand-new weapon. At your command, a sailor pushes down on a set of bellows, blasting air into a furnace at the prow of your ship. Above the furnace is the brass figure of a lion. As the sailor squeezes the bellows, a stream of orange flame shoots out of the lion's mouth, terrifying the enemy soldiers and setting fire to their ship. It's the first demonstration of Greek fire!

This is unfair!

No, it's Greek fire!

What's in it?

Not telling you.

MYSTERY WEAPON. No one knows what fuel was used in these Byzantine flamethrowers (the recipe was a closely guarded secret), but it may have been crude oil mixed with resin.

FIRE IN WARFARE. Since ancient times, fire has been a weapon. Burning projectiles were hurled over besieged city walls, and fireships were sent to destroy enemy navies.

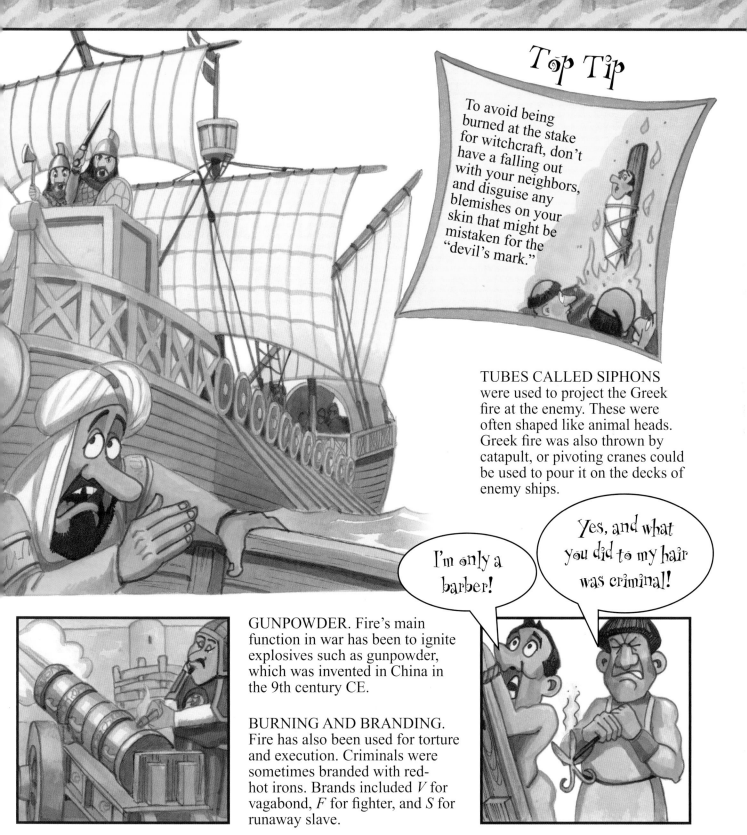

Top Tip

To avoid being burned at the stake for witchcraft, don't have a falling out with your neighbors, and disguise any blemishes on your skin that might be mistaken for the "devil's mark."

TUBES CALLED SIPHONS were used to project the Greek fire at the enemy. These were often shaped like animal heads. Greek fire was also thrown by catapult, or pivoting cranes could be used to pour it on the decks of enemy ships.

I'm only a barber!

Yes, and what you did to my hair was criminal!

GUNPOWDER. Fire's main function in war has been to ignite explosives such as gunpowder, which was invented in China in the 9th century CE.

BURNING AND BRANDING. Fire has also been used for torture and execution. Criminals were sometimes branded with red-hot irons. Brands included *V* for vagabond, *F* for fighter, and *S* for runaway slave.

Are You All Set for Steam?

ornwall, England, 1712: You are assisting the inventor Thomas Newcomen with his new steam engine. Your job is to keep the fire burning in the boiler. The fire will turn water in the cylinder into steam. Cold water is then injected into the cylinder to condense the steam back into water. This creates a vacuum that pulls the piston down. When the fire turns the water to steam again, it pushes the piston up. This up-and-down motion drives a pump that will clear water from a coal or tin mine. You are very excited by this new engine and the idea that fire—and steam—can produce power that humans can use.

Beam

It does 12 strokes per minute, and it can raise 10 imperial gallons (45.5 L) of water at each stroke from a depth of 165 feet (50 m).

Piston

Linkage to water pump at bottom of mine

Cylinder

Boiler

JAMES WATT (left) improved Newcomen's engine by creating a separate chamber where steam could be cooled. His engine also changed up-and-down motion into circular motion to turn a wheel.

Top Tip

Coke is the best fuel for smelting iron in a blast furnace. Coal is cheaper, but it contains sulfur, which will make your iron brittle.

Coke

Furnace —

Bellows —

FACTORIES. By the early 1800s, steam power was being used to drive machinery in enormous factories. It marked the start of the Industrial Revolution. Factory workers had to do long shifts in poor conditions for low wages.

I work 68 hours a week.

Wouldn't you if you were on fire?

Why is it moving so fast?

1779 cast-iron bridge at Ironbridge, Shropshire, England

TRANSPORTATION. By the 1820s, steam locomotives were moving goods and people on land, and steamships were replacing sails.

ELECTRICITY. Today, many power stations still burn coal to make steam. This steam drives turbines to create electricity.

COAL AND IRON. The fires of the Industrial Revolution burned coal. Coke, a product of coal, fueled blast furnaces that smelted iron for buildings, machines, bridges, and much more.

25

Could You Conceive of a Car?

It is now 1863. You are inventor Etienne Lenoir, embarking on the world's first road trip by motorized carriage in Paris, France. Your carriage attracts a lot of startled looks from passersby as it pops and burbles along.

It travels just a little faster than walking pace, and you must stop frequently to make small repairs. Yet you complete your 14-mile (22-kilometer) journey in three hours, proving to the world that there are other ways of getting around, aside from horses and steam power.

LENOIR'S "CAR" was powered by an internal combustion engine (see opposite page). The engine burned coal gas, ignited by what Lenoir called "jumping sparks."

You are frightening my horse!

Soon there will be no more need for horses, monsieur!

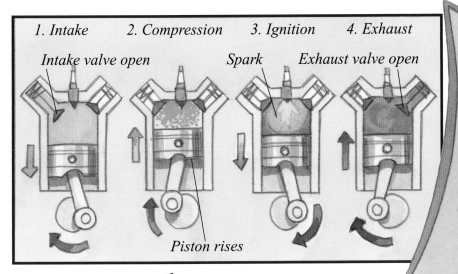

1. Intake   2. Compression   3. Ignition   4. Exhaust

Intake valve open   Spark   Exhaust valve open

Piston rises

You Can Do It!

When a rocket engine burns fuel, it forces out hot exhaust gases at high speed. This pushes the rocket in the opposite direction. Exactly the same thing happens when you let the air out of a balloon.

FFFFFFFF

Internal Combustion Engine

AT THE HEART of the engine is a cylinder containing a piston.
1. INTAKE: The piston starts at the bottom of the cylinder. The intake valve opens, letting in a mix of fuel (usually gasoline) and air.
2. COMPRESSION: The piston moves back up to compress the fuel/air mixture.

3. IGNITION: The spark plug ignites the fuel. The explosion drives the piston down.
4. EXHAUST: When the piston reaches the bottom of the cylinder, another valve opens, letting out the exhaust.
This whole process is called the four-stroke cycle.

HOW CARS MOVE.
A connecting rod joins the piston to a crankshaft, which turns the piston's up-and-down motion into rotary motion, giving power and movement to the car's wheels.

FIRE IN THE SKY. The internal combustion engine soon filled our streets with cars, trucks, motorbikes, and many other vehicles. Powered flight was achieved in 1903.

Ah! This is fun! Now, where are the brakes?

Biplane ca. 1914

Squawk!

Can You Forecast the Future of Fire?

One hundred years in the future, you arrive home on your hover scooter. A scanner checks your identity, and the door slides open. "Light!" you say, and the hallway lights up, powered by solar energy collected in space.

It's chilly, so you request some "Heat!" The room is warmed by geothermal energy from deep underground. Then you remember something. You put on a pair of glasses, powered by your body movements. "Mom!" you say, and a moment later, she's there on a screen before your eyes. You smile at her...

FIRE WITHIN US. Sunlight helps plants grow. We eat plants (and the animals that feed on them). So, in an indirect way, our bodies convert fire (from the Sun) into energy. In the future we may use our bodies' movements to power small gadgets such as intelligent spectacles.

Happy birthday, Mom!

28

FIRE FROM SPACE. We could harvest the Sun's energy with space-based solar panels, convert this to electricity, and beam it back to Earth. The panels would work all the time, because there's no nighttime in space, and no clouds to block out the sunlight.

HYDROGEN (right) could be the fuel of the future. An engine burning hydrogen produces almost no pollution. But obtaining hydrogen from substances such as natural gas requires heat. So fire will remain important to us for a while—even when we're driving around in hover cars!

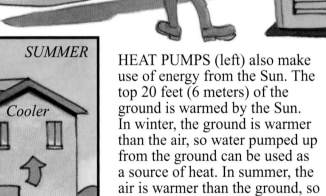

WINTER

SUMMER

Warmer

Cooler

Cold water

Warm water

Heat pump

Warm water

Cool water

HEAT PUMPS (left) also make use of energy from the Sun. The top 20 feet (6 meters) of the ground is warmed by the Sun. In winter, the ground is warmer than the air, so water pumped up from the ground can be used as a source of heat. In summer, the air is warmer than the ground, so water from under the ground can be used for cooling.

The interior of Earth is extremely hot, and in some parts of the world it is possible to generate energy from the heat inside the planet. This is called geothermal energy.

Glossary

Adobe Sun-dried brick made of clay, sometimes mixed with other materials.

Alloy A metal made by combining two or more metallic elements, to make it stronger or more resistant to corrosion.

Anvil A heavy iron or steel block on which metal is hammered and shaped.

Backfire A fire started on purpose to stop a wildfire by depriving it of fuel.

Bellows A device for blowing air into a fire to make it burn more strongly.

Blast furnace A high-temperature furnace (oven) for smelting metals.

Boiler A fuel-burning container used for heating water.

Byzantine Belonging to a Greek-speaking empire in Asia that lasted from the 4th century CE until 1453.

Cast iron An alloy of iron and carbon that can be cast in a mold. It is hard but brittle.

Cob A mixture of compressed clay and straw used for building walls.

Coke A fuel made by heating coal in the absence of air.

Condense To change from a gas to a liquid.

Cordwood Wood cut to uniform lengths, used in wall building when laid crosswise with masonry or cob.

Crankshaft A rod inside an internal combustion engine, which is turned by the motion of the pistons.

Crucible A ceramic or metal container in which metals are melted.

Exhaust Waste gases expelled from an engine in the course of its operation.

Firebreak A strip of open ground that stops a wildfire by depriving it of fuel.

Fireship A ship loaded with burning material and explosives, set adrift to burn enemy ships.

Forge A furnace or hearth for melting or working metal; also, a smith's workshop, or smithy.

Geothermal energy Heat energy that comes from inside Earth.

Hearth A fireplace used for heating and for cooking food.

Heat pump A device that moves heat from one place to another.

Ignition Setting something on fire.

Industrial Revolution The period in the 18th and 19th centuries when many new technologies were developed, especially steam power.

Internal combustion engine An engine in which the fuel (usually gasoline or diesel oil) is burned inside the cylinder, not in a separate boiler.

Kiln A furnace or oven for firing pottery.

Mesopotamia An area of the ancient Middle East, consisting of modern Iraq and parts of neighboring countries.

Persia The ancient name for Iran.

Piston Part of an engine: a disk that is moved up and down inside a cylinder to turn energy into motion.

Rotary motion Circular motion, like the turning of a wheel.

Smelting The extraction of a metal from its ore by a process that involves heating and melting.

Turbine A machine for producing power, in which a rotor is made to revolve by a fast-moving flow of fluid.

Vacuum A space or container from which the air has been completely or partly removed.

Valve A device for controlling the passage of fluid through a pipe or duct.

Wattle and daub A building material that consists of interwoven sticks and twigs covered with mud or clay.

Wildfire A large, destructive fire that spreads quickly over forest, woodland, or brush.

Index

Top Deadly Fires

1. Great Kanto Earthquake and Fire, Japan, September 1, 1923

Following a massive earthquake, Tokyo was ravaged by a fire that killed around 142,000 people and destroyed 570,000 homes.

2. *Doña Paz* collision, Philippines, December 20, 1987

When the passenger ferry *Doña Paz* collided with a fuel tanker, MT *Vector*, fire spread quickly through both ships, killing more than 4,000 people.

3. Great Fire of Southwark, London, England, July 12, 1212

Not as famous as the 1666 Fire of London, but far more devastating, this fire left around 3,000 dead and about a third of the city in ruins.

4. Great San Francisco Earthquake and Fire, April 1906

The earthquake and the fire that followed it killed 3,000 people and destroyed more than 500 city blocks, leaving half the city's population homeless.

5. Jesuit Church, Santiago, Chile, December 8, 1863

An oil lamp set a painting ablaze during a service. With the doors closed, the worshippers were trapped. Around 2,500 died.

6. Halifax explosion, Nova Scotia, Canada, December 6, 1917

SS *Imo* collided with steam freighter SS *Mont Blanc*, loaded with up to 3,000 tons of explosives, in Halifax Harbor. The explosion leveled half of Halifax and killed 2,000 people.

7. Peshtigo, Wisconsin, October 8, 1871

A devastating forest fire consumed 2,400 square miles (6,200 square kilometers), destroyed two billion trees, and took 1,200 to 2,400 lives.

Fire as a Symbol

Fire has played a key role in the development of human civilization, so it's not surprising that it has been an important symbol in human culture and religion.

Fire is one of the four elements in ancient Greek philosophy—the others being water, air, and earth. The Greeks thought that everything in the universe was made up of these four elements. Fire, they believed, gives us qualities such as energy and passion.

The ancient Romans worshipped both the hearth and the forge. Vesta was the goddess of the hearth. She was served by the Vestal Virgins, who tended a sacred flame in their temple in Rome. The god of the forge was Vulcan, who looked after blacksmiths and protected against accidental fires in cities. Both Greeks and Romans killed and burned animals on an altar as a sacrifice to their gods.

In Hinduism, Agni is the god of fire. In Zoroastrianism, fire is considered a symbol of purity, righteousness, and truth. In the Old Testament of the Bible, fire appears at crucial moments, such as in the forms of the burning bush and the pillar of fire. In the New Testament, the Holy Spirit appears as tongues of flame.

Fire continues to be an important symbol today. Bonfires form part of celebrations around the world. Candles are used in religious ceremonies, and eternal flames are used to remind us of significant events. The Olympic flame is the most famous of these.

Did You Know?

The Founding Fathers of the United States were firefighters. Benjamin Franklin founded the first volunteer firefighting service in 1736 in Philadelphia. George Washington, Samuel Adams, and Thomas Jefferson were also volunteer firefighters.

Every 52 years, when their calendar completed a cycle, the Aztecs would extinguish every fire in their empire. A new fire would be started on the opened chest of a sacrificial victim.

• The Melanophila beetle seeks out forest fires using infrared radiation sensors. It lays its eggs in dead trees, because they lack protective mechanisms like sap to prevent larvae from burrowing.

Fire can consume all the oxygen in a room. Many people trapped in burning buildings die from lack of oxygen.

• A candle flame typically burns at around 1,800°F (1,000°C).

• Earth is the only known planet where fire can burn.

• The amount of oxygen affects the color of a flame. Low-oxygen flames are yellow; high-oxygen flames burn blue.

• Haystacks, compost heaps, old newspaper, and even pistachio nuts have been known to spontaneously burst into flame.

• An underground coal seam near Wingen, Australia, has been burning continuously for an estimated 6,000 years.